Portfolio Collection volume 3
Caroline Broadhead

TELOS

1 | invisible people
1990

... without a memory there is no possibility of knowing who you are.
———— Caroline Broadhead

Authors: Jeremy Theophilus, Caroline Broadhead
Editor: Matthew Koumis
Graphic Designer: You. Kobayashi
Reprographics: Fotoriproduzioni Grafiche, Verona
Printed in Italy by Grafiche AZ

Published by
Telos Art Publishing
PO Box 125, Winchester
SO23 7UJ
England
telephone: +44(0)1962 864546
facsimile: +44(0)1962 864727
e-mail: editorial@telos.net
URL: www.arttextiles.com

Photo Credits:
Peter Mackertich and Caroline Broadhead, page 4
Gary Kirkham, front and back cover, pages 6, 9, 24, 26, 27, 28, 30, 33, 34
Hugo Glendenning, pages 11, 36, 37, 38, 39, 40, 42
Nigel Hillier, pages 22, 25, 29, 32
Caroline Broadhead, pages 16, 17, 18

Acknowledgements

Special thanks to Middlesex University.

The authors and publisher wish to acknowledge the contribution made by *A Short History of the Shadow*, by Victor Stoichita, published by Reaktion Books, 1997.

'The Waiting Game' (pp. 36-42) was a collaboration between the artist and Angela Woodhouse, with dancers Marcia Pook and Fabio Santos, at Upnor Castle, Kent, in 1997.

Caroline Broadhead is represented by Barratt Marsden Gallery, London.

With many thanks to all those who have helped in the production of this book, including Adriana Mosqueira, Ian Chalmers, Sue Leahy, Katherine James, Alessandra, Simone and Ermanno.

Front cover illustration: suspend (2001),tulle, thread
Back cover: still light (1999), elastane, talc

Contents

2 | double dresses
| 2000

Material, space, and color are the main aspects of visual art. Everyone knows that there is material that can be picked up and sold, but no one sees space and color. Two of the main aspects of art are invisible: the basic nature of art is invisible. The integrity of visual art is not seen (Donald Judd: *Some Aspects of Color in General, and Red and Black in Particular,*1993).

It is this challenge to make the invisible visible, within the broadest interpretation of the word, that gives the practice of visual art its driving force. Judd's flatly delivered commentary also implies that the visual artist needs to involve a number of senses and mental processes in order to communicate. More than ever before, in employing a diversity of media and processes the artist can transcend the conventions of category and tradition; in Caroline Broadhead's case, however, this transcendence expands rather than negates the impact of tradition.

The earliest attempts by wo/man to fix the mysteries of space and colour have been described by Pliny: *The question as to the origin of the art of painting is uncertain... but all agree that it began with tracing an outline around a man's shadow and consequently that pictures were originally done in this way...* (Pliny: *Natural History*, XXXV, 15).

Clearly this was not in itself a fully creative act, merely an image of a shadow, in effect nothing more than a copy of a copy, but with a strong resonance to working methods of artists across the centuries and no less relevant today. Caroline Broadhead's interest in the shadow and its potential for revisiting and questioning issues of perception, transformation and reality can therefore be seen to continue a familiar tradition.

A whole system of symbolism is attached to the shadow in Greek and Egyptian cultures: by re-presenting the shadow's shape in two/three dimensional form, a constant presence is given to the absent shadow's creator (the loved one); the new image becomes then an object of reverence, and acquires a cult status. The Greeks symbolically linked shadow, soul and a person's double. The Egyptians first visualised the soul (ka) as a clear shadow, a coloured projection, but aerial to the individual, reproducing every one of his features. The black shadow (khaibit) was considered to be the double of man, an externalisation of his being. On death, the function of the double is taken over by the ka as well as the statue and the mummy. In this context the vertical as opposed to the recumbent (the living as opposed to the dead) is an important distinction, particularly as it leads to the development of sculpture as a distinct artform.

In 1992, Caroline Broadhead drew a line under her work to that date and turned to face the world with an open mind: both liberated and exposed she spent a year thinking, drawing and photographing, culminating in a period spent in Italy, where she read Dante and began to engage with the shadow as a theme.

She also encountered a seminal text on the subject: A Short History of the Shadow (Victor I Stoichita, Reaktion Books, 1997), from which some of this introduction has been drawn. Two frescos discussed in the book have also become important in understanding Caroline Broadhead's current thinking.

The first (illus. p.14) is called 'The Origin of Painting' (1573), from the Casa Vasari in Florence, in which Gyges of Lydia is shown kneeling against the wall onto which his shadow has been thrown by a lamp, and is drawing an outline of himself on the wall with a piece of coal. In this one image Vasari, the (first) art historian, seeks to combine the shadow theory of the origin of art with the mirror theory that was adopted from Ovid's story of Narcissus in his Metamorphoses: an integration of the conceptual with the erotic.

In the second (illus. p.15), Masaccio's 'St Peter Healing the Sick', 1427-8, Brancacci Chapel, S. Maria del Carmine, Florence, depicts a passage in the Acts of the Apostles: ... in the hope that even the shadow of Peter, as he passed by, might fall upon one of them here and there, and so they would be healed of their infirmities.

Recent commentaries on this event confirm the ancient, magical concept of the shadow as an external manifestation of the soul which, in the context of this particular Saint, would appear to have supernatural powers inherent in merely passing by the sick and infirm. In blocking out the light, the healing presence of Peter is miraculously transferred through the shadow onto those he passed.

Dante, too, uses the shadow as a means of confirming life. His companion Virgil lacks sufficient physical presence to break the sun's rays, leaving the darkness of the author:

Fire-red behind our backs the sun was pouring
Light on the slope before us, broken where
I blocked the rays, my shadowy outline scoring

Black on the ground – I whipped about in fear,
Abandoned, as I thought, beholding how
I, and I only, made a darkness there.

(Dante: *Purgatory Canto*, 3,16-21,
translated by Dorothy L Sayers, Penguin)

It is striking however that, in Masaccio's painting, the bulk of the Saint's presence is indicated by the voluminous folds of his garments, themselves shaded; the all-important shadow itself is barely indicated as anything more than a smudge across the ground.

Both paintings are heavily symbolic whilst at the same time apparently simple descriptions of simple acts. The one refers to a relationship between light, the earth and the human body; the other to a more developed cultural narrative in which natural phenomena are imbued with meaning. In revisiting these early works, Caroline Broadhead is grounding her own practice in Western canons of visual art and philosophy, as well as reminding us that a linear perspective on history is and has to be constantly challenged by artists. Nothing is sacred but, equally, nothing is that new...

There is a third image to which Caroline Broadhead has been drawn *(illus. p.15)*, that of George Cruikshank's 1827 engraving for Peter Schlemihl: 'The Man in Grey Offers Peter Schlemihl his Shadow in Exchange for his Soul'. A variant on the Faust myth, this story concerns a young man who does a deal with the Devil in exchanging his shadow for gold. In a subsequent negotiation the Devil offers to return his shadow in exchange for his soul. In this engraving Cruikshank has shown the Devil with both his own and Schlemihl's shadows, together forming on the ground an almost complete rectangle with a pronounced diagonal.

It is also interesting to note that other interpretations of this story show the shadow being rolled up like a piece of cloth. We might also remember that Peter Pan had his shadow sewed back on by Wendy. There is a long history that assigns both a particular physical and psychological presence to the shadow.

Caroline Broadhead's drawings are spare, like diagrams; her photographs of the shadow *(pp.18-19)* are more inclusive, more suggestive of place and specific architecture, indeed are more about surface, texture and colour. They are also about confusing the eye: distance, proportion, depth are all challenged whilst at the same time acknowledging the presence of the artist: the shadow is herself.

Shadows define an architectural space, demand a surface, an edge, suggest a presence, touch and then move on in parallel, but they cannot be themselves without suggesting a progenitor, an other that is also the same. In working through this theme, Caroline Broadhead has found a context for textile where the technique is deliberately constrained by the idea. Using a rigour that excludes all but that which is essential to the construction and the meaning, she imbues the unremarkable with a specificity that is, at the same time, barely present.

We might think of these works as the ghostly that are more than reflected light. We talk about them as recognisable objects with a clearly defined function, they are dresses, costumes; they define the feminine and confront the masculine; they hang, they are suspended, they express a range of emotions from the yearning to the compliant; they contain less physically than emotionally; they challenge perspective and surface by playing games with light.

There is a kind of repetitive calligraphy that operates through Caroline Broadhead's work: sharp lines that support and direct the fabric; openings top and bottom, and one each side: tightly drawn round neck and wrists, less constrained across the hem. The use of line in space: the darkness of the sharp fold or the delineating edge/end of a sleeve/hem. Where is the end and the beginning? Where light passes through unhindered:

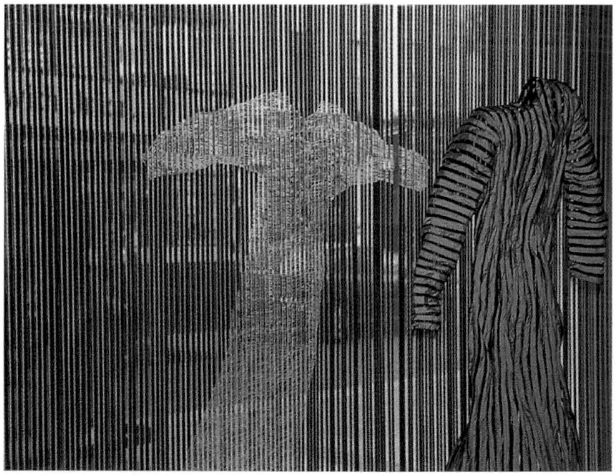

White
what moves us,
without weight
what we exchange.
White and Light:
let it drift
(Paul Celan: 'White and Light', 1959)

By anchoring the shadow by means of a shaded shape, the memory of a presence/pose is held, but in these works a conversation is set up between the real and the negative other, in which both the two and three dimensonal seem to merge and the shadow can be seen through the transparent costume: how can this be?

3 | line drawings
| 1999

9

There is a fascinating tension in Caroline Broadhead's work that exists around the principle of gravity. Suspended fabric: a fiction that deliberately sets out to confuse the eye, both in terms of the engineering of presence and in the translucence of material. Dresses when worn don't touch the floor, therefore why should these? They are suspended within the breadth of human proportion: we recognise them as familiar, we fill them (or do we?) with our likenesses but do they really reference the body in any specific way?

By hanging/floating before us they become disconnected and inhabit a gravity-free zone, aided by our own willing suspension of disbelief, as the fabric moves/is moved and fixed in ways that indicate a volume within that is articulated from without, a textile architecture rather than a corporeal. Caroline Broadhead poses a series of open questions to the spectator, about the nature of inner and outer space, the contained and the seemingly endless, as well as the more everyday issues of clothing and costume's relationship with the human body.

Another side to Caroline Broadhead's work involves responding to a specific site, and collaborating with artists working in other media. In 'the waiting game' *(illus. pp. 36-42)* for instance, a dominant theme is one of restraint, holding down/back/under, as if the strong presence of history anchors any attempt to move freely. Even when forms are suspended, the architecture bears down upon or contains their apparent mobility: the weighting game?

In engaging with a choreographer and dancer, Caroline Broadhead steps through that fine line between the costume as shape, container, surface, and the costume as activated through human movement. But even here she is able to mediate that tension, as the costume becomes a fabric skin to the room in which it is performed, and the spectators interact through having to step on this carpet/costume. This more direct and time-limited relationship with an audience allows Caroline Broadhead to experiment with differing readings of textile, as well as testing her own ideas in the context of a creative team.

In talking about the way she works, Caroline Broadhead describes a process of assembling different ingredients, in and through which she searches for those transformative elements that will combine to provide the right mix. A key issue for her is the insistence on using ordinary materials and techniques: keeping it simple so that the end result has an even greater impact, the journey is far richer.

She refers to 'preparing the potential' through a process of playing with materials in the studio, seeking out and/or waiting for those moments of clear possibility. She also confesses to a preference for starting rather than finishing, echoed here in George Steiner's recent study on the nature of creation: ... *the artist's reiterated sense of frustration, of sorrow in respect of the finished or published oeuvre; each of whose components is an inevitably reductive, diminished articulation of far richer and more inward possibilities.*
George Steiner: *Grammars of Creation*, Faber, 2001

Decisions for her are almost always motivated by external deadlines, where the public presentation is a conclusion, what she calls 'an anxious release'. Inevitably there is always an inherent sense of risk: whether the work can/will be finished, and indeed whether it will be the 'right' conclusion. Even allowing for the deliberately simple range of materials and processes, each installation is finely constructed, requiring patience and a clear head.

The body of work Caroline Broadhead has produced over the past ten years has been clearly about finding ways to capture and define those elements of the visual that are least definable. She chooses to work through textile, but in its least solid form, where she maximises the open weave and the least reflective qualities of the material. She continues to explore the nature of the human presence, both in its physicality and in its memory, and treads that very fine line between the breath and its absence. In a very real sense, however, she is for the breath, appropriately given metaphor in this anecdote from *The Golden Bough*:

At a funeral in China, when the lid is about to be placed on the coffin, most of the bystanders, with the exception of the nearest kin, retire a few steps or even retreat to another room, for a person's health is believed to be endangered by allowing his shadow to be enclosed in a coffin... the gravediggers and coffin-bearers attach their shadows firmly to their persons by tying a strip of cloth tightly around their waists.
James Frazer: 'The Golden Bough', 1890

Jeremy Theophilus

13 | the waiting game
| 1997

Inspirations

windows and shadows

Vasari
The Origin of Painting (1573)

George Cruikshank
*The Man in Grey Offers Peter Schlemihl's
Shadow in Exchange for his Soul* (1827)

Masaccio
St Peter Healing the Sick (1427-8)

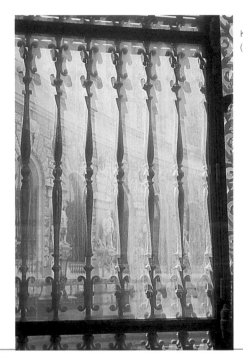

Kunsthistorisch Museum window, Vienna
(photos by Caroline Broadhead)

Windows

Studio window in floodlight, Vienna

rainy window

danger shadow – falling through
photos by Caroline Broadhead

danger shadow – falling in

danger shadow – falling under

Colour Plates

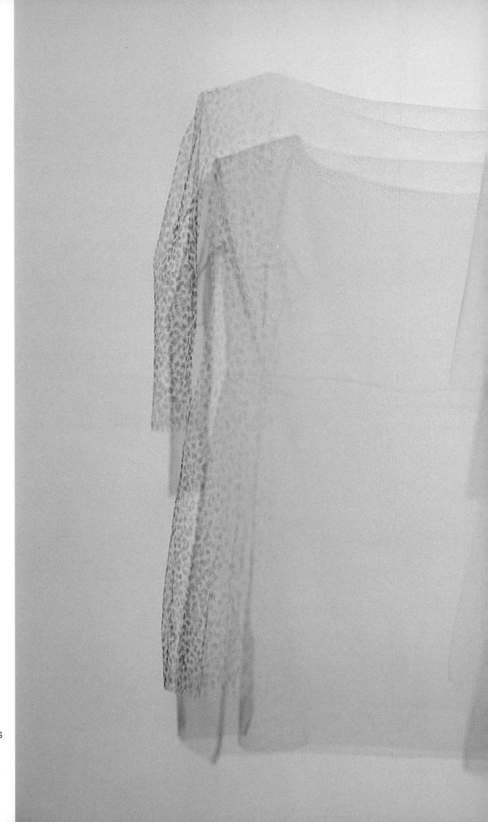

4 | overlapping dresses
| 2001

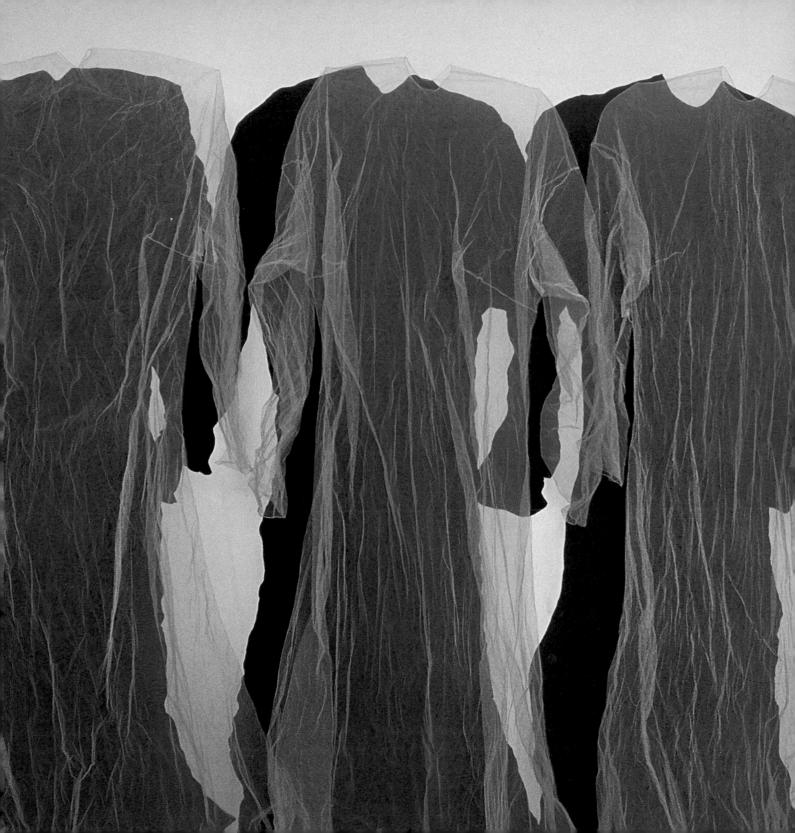

6 | halves
| 2001

left:
5 | back to the wall
| detail
| 2001

above and right:

2 | double dresses
2000

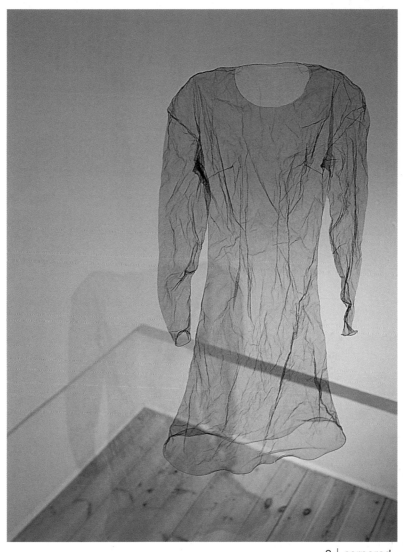

8 | cornered
| 2001

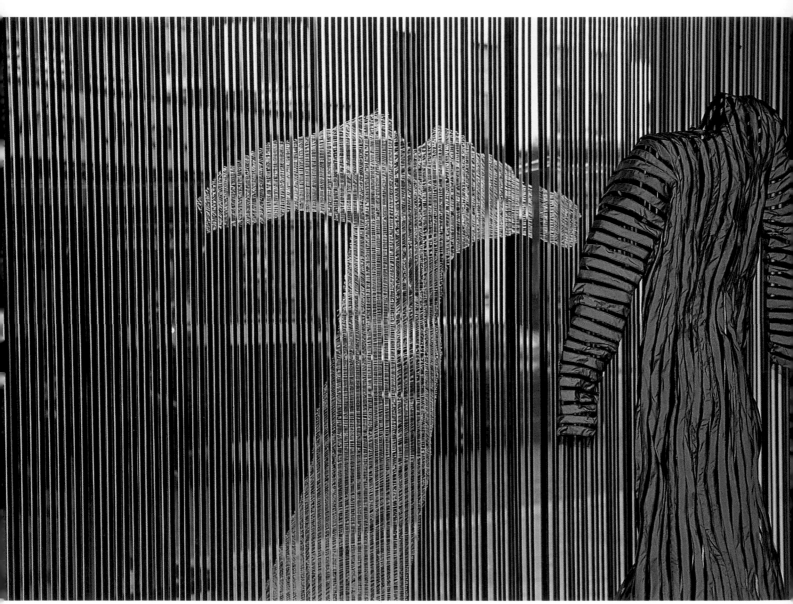

3 | line drawings
| 1999

9 | invisible dress
1998

10 | web
2001

right:
11 | suspend
2001

12 | still light
1999

14 | dress in the bread oven (II)
 | 1997

right:
15 | suit of armour
 | 1997

16 | bastion scenes
Upnor Castle, Kent

17 | the waiting game
| 1997

Biography

Caroline Broadhead

Awards
1997   Winner, Jerwood Prize for Applied Arts: Textiles
2000   Year of the Artist Award for *veilsafe* with Claire Russ

Selected Solo Exhibitions
2001   'New Work', Barratt Marsden Gallery, London

'Chiaroscuro', Mid Pennine Arts, Burnley

2000   'Between Light and Dark', Galerie Ra, Amsterdam

1999   'Bodyscape: Caroline Broadhead', Angel Row Gallery, Nottingham (tour)

Selected Group Exhibitions
2001   'Caroline Broadhead, Carol McNicoll, Irene Nordli, Sigurd Bronger'
Kunsthall, Bergen, Norway

'Crossing Borders', Sorlandet Museum, Kristiansand, Norway

2000   'Art Textiles 2', Bury St Edmunds

'Ikons of Identity', Midlands Art Centre, Birmingham (tour)

'Three Decades', The London Institute Gallery, London

'Het Versierde Ego', Koning Sabiolazaal, Antwerp, Belgium

'Mensch Design', Museum fur Kunst und Gewerbe, Hamburg

'Special Exhibit', SOFA, Chicago

1999   'Textures of Memory', Angel Row Gallery, Nottingham (tour)

'Lifecycles', Galerie fur Zeitgenossische Kunst, Leipzig

'Weaving the World', Yokohama Museum of Art

'Catching the Light', MAC bus, Fife

'Flexible 3' (invited artist) tour: Austria, Poland, Netherlands, England, Germany

1998   'Addressing the Century', 100 years of Art & Fashion, Hayward Gallery, London (tour)

'Beyond Material', Oriel Mostyn, Llandudno (tour)

'Tempered', Fabrica, Brighton

1996   'Under Construction', Crafts Council Gallery, London (tour)

1993	'On the Edge', Crafts Council Gallery, London (tour)
1990	'Three Ways of Seeing', retrospective with Fred Baier and Richard Slee, Crafts Council, London
1986	'Conceptual Clothing', Ikon Gallery, Birmingham and tour

Selected Performances

2000	'veilsafe', collaboration with Claire Russ, Castle Vale, Birmingham and tour
1997	'the waiting game', collaboration with Angela Woodhouse, Upnor Castle, Kent
1995	'unlaced grace', collaboration with Claire Russ, Mill Arts Centre, Banbury

Teaching

1997, 99	International Sommerakademie, Salzburg
1996 -	Goldsmiths College, University of London, BA Hons, Textiles
1986 -	Middlesex University, BA Hons, Jewellery

Residency

| 1998 | Three month Artist-in Residence scheme, Vienna |

Selected Publications

1999	*Art Textiles of the World: GB* vol 2, Telos Art Publishing, ed. Dr J Harris	ISBN 0952626764
	50 Years of British Creativity, Michael Racburn, Thames & Hudson	ISBN 0500019061
	Ideas in the Making, Practice into Theory, ed. P Johnson, University of East Anglia	ISBN 187014581X
	The Crafts in Britain in the 20th Century, Tanya Harrod, Yale University Press	ISBN 0300077807
1992	*New Textiles*, Chloe Colchester, Thames and Hudson	ISBN 0500277370
1990	*Caroline Broadhead in Studio*, John Houston, Bellew Publishing / Crafts Council	ISBN 0947792481
1985	*The New Jewelry*, Peter Dormer and Ralph Turner, Thames and Hudson	ISBN 0500277745

Work in Public Collections

Worshipful Company of Goldsmiths, London

Crafts Council, London

Castle Museum, Norwich

Stedelijk Museum, Amsterdam

Gemeentelijke Van Reekumgalerij, Apeldoorn, Netherlands

National Museum of Scotland

Shipley Art Gallery, Gateshead

Israel Museum, Jerusalem

County Museum, Middlesbrough, Cleveland

Crafts Board of Australia Council, Sydney

Nederlands Kostuummuseum (Haags Gemeentemuseum), The Hague

North West Arts Association, Manchester

Museum of Modern Art, Kyoto

Bristol City Art Gallery

Wakefield City Art Gallery

Castle Museum, Nottingham

Contemporary Collection, V & A Museum, London

Kunstmuseum, Bayreuth

Extended recorded interview, National Life Story Collection: British Library, London

Trondheim Museum, Norway

Index of illustrated works

Other titles in this series

Vol 3: Caroline Broadhead (UK)
by Jeremy Theophilus
Shadows, windows, invisibility...
examine some of the inspirational
threads animating Britain's winner of
the Jerwood Prize for Textiles.
ISBN 1902015231

Vol 4: Chika Ohgi (Japan)
by Keiko Kawashima
Be enchanted by one of Kyoto's finest
artists working in installations with paper.
She composes her work using space itself
as an equal presence.
ISBN 1902015258

Vol 5: Anne Marie Power (Australia)
by Dr Juliette Peers
Textile artist, papermaker and sculptor,
Power plays upon the issues of cultural
trafficking and influences between
continent and continent.
ISBN 1902015266

Vol 6: Anne Wilson (USA)
by Tim Porges and Hattie Gordon
This important American artist uses human
hair, table linens and hand-stitching to probe
poignant personal memories and histories,
as well as evoking a subtle sense of landscape.
ISBN 1902015223

Vol 7: Alice Kettle (UK)
by Dr Jennifer Harris
Get up close and intimate with probably
the largest machine embroideries in the world
dating from 1997–2002, including a move
to landscape.
ISBN 1902015312

**visit www.arttextiles.com to order any of our titles
online or to view a list of our international stockists**

Vol 8: Helen Lancaster (Australia)
by Carolyn Skinner
The perilous fragility of nature, beautifully depicted
by an outstanding conceptual environmentalist using
embroidery and fabric manipulation.
ISBN 1902015290

Vol 9: Kay Lawrence (Australia)
by Dr Diana Wood Conroy
One of the world's top tapestry weavers, her recent
work negotiates issues about identity in textures
ranging from minimal to lush, from sensuous to spiky.
ISBN 1902015282

Vol 10: Joan Livingstone (USA)
by Gerry Craig
Livingstone's powerful installations incorporate felt,
stitch and epoxy resin. Professor of Fiber and Material
Studies at the School of the Art Institute, Chicago, she
is one of America's most important fiber sculptors.
ISBN 1902015274

Vol 11: Marian Smit (Netherlands)
by Marjolein v.d. Stoep
1st Prize winner in Third International Paper Triennal,
Switzerland, 1999. "Work of great simplicity
combining technique and poetry."
ISBN 1902015320

Vol 12: Chiyoko Tanaka (Japan)
by Lesley Millar
Tanaka's prized weavings are in public collections
around the world. A leading light from Kyoto,
her work is breathtaking and awe-inspiring.
ISBN 190201524X

still available:
Vol 1: Jilly Edwards (UK)
by Lene Bragger and Melanie Cook
ISBN 1902015207

Vol 2: Marian Bijlenga (Netherlands)
by Jack Lenor Larsen and Gert Staal
ISBN 1902015215